GOOD·OLD·DAYS®

Live It Again™

1941

Dear Friends,

Whenever the year 1941 is mentioned, most of those familiar with American history immediately think of the infamous surprise air strike by Japanese forces that catapulted the United States into World War II. Certainly that event and the subsequent declaration of war upon the Axis powers of Japan, Germany and Italy overshadow the year.

Almost immediately war preparations shifted into high gear. Manufacturers were already refitting industrial plants to produce the weapons of war. The first War Bonds drive saw millions of Americans putting their money where their hearts were. A brand new USO—United Service Organization—began taking care of the social and recreational needs of an ever-expanding military. And the new cars rolling off the Motown lines in 1941 would be the last produced for the next five years.

"Ready Teddy" was the last visage carved on Mount Rushmore.

But so much more happened in 1941 than that tragic Sunday, Dec. 7, that has come to define the year.

The year began with the inauguration of a beloved president—Franklin Delano Roosevelt—to an unprecedented third term. President Roosevelt would go on to win a fourth term, but he would not live to see the end of the war, dying of a stroke in the spring of 1945.

Another Roosevelt's face was in the news in 1941 as well—but President Theodore Roosevelt's image was on a mountaintop in South Dakota. "Ready Teddy" was the last visage carved on Mount Rushmore. Work ceased on the monument on Oct. 31, 1941, after federal funds dried up in anticipation of the inevitable war.

This yearbook through photographs and words captures all of that and so much more. Come with us as we live again the joys and the tears that marked this special year. Join us as we take a passionate look at the heart and soul of the year that was 1941.

Contents

SHELL

JULY SERVICE TIP

Vacation soon? Drive in for Shell-ubrication—a "Thoro-Fast" serv-ice that puts the right lubricant in the right spots in the right amount.

REPRINTED WITH PERMISSION OF MICHELIN NORTH AMERICA

REPRINTED WITH PERMISSION FROM GENERAL MOTORS COMPANY

Everyday Life

Winter activities

In 1941, winter brought a mixture of creative fun and lots of hard work. Keeping warm often meant early rising to fire up the furnace. Daily chores involved chopping wood and carrying it into the house.

There was no easy way to clear walks and driveways other than the muscle power of shoveling snow. Often, there was work involved with pleasure, such as cleaning off the local pond in order to ice skate or play hockey.

Those participating in winter sports often made their own skis and hockey sticks. Sometimes the moments of frolic were enhanced by a cup of hot cocoa and homemade cookies.

COURTESY OF THE DOW CHEMICAL COMPANY

Skiing involved patting down snow on a local hillside in order to slicken it for an afternoon of fun with the neighborhood gang.

REPRINTED WITH PERMISSION FROM GENERAL MOTORS COMPANY

uilding snowmen was often a creative art involving eighborhood competition to see who could construct he most creative and decorated masterpiece.

© 1941 SEPS

© 1941 SEPS

"Is Brattleboro still four inches of powder on a light breakable crust, do you know?"

Mercury 8

Chevrolet

Cars of 1941

One of the most drastic shifts in the history of the American economy occurred by the end of 1941 when the decision was made to stop automobile production. Many of the domestic automotive plants were converted to military production. The year prior to shutdown, 1940, United States manufacturers produced a total of 4,680,000 cars.

The Department of War came up with the idea for a one-quarter ton, four-wheel drive military vehicle called the Jeep. By July of 1941, the War Department asked manufacturer, Willys-Overland, to fulfill an order for 16,000 Jeeps.

Cadillac Sixty-One Five-Passenger Coupe

The Finest Lincolns Ever Built

Lincoln Zephyr V-12

Buick Special Four-Door Sedan Model 47

Chrysler

Ford

Plymouth Convertible Coupe

Pontiac Custom "Torpedo" Six Station Wagon

Hudson

Studebaker Land Cruiser

Dodge

Cars of 1941

Car sales in 1941 were just as much about promoting ads as they were the vehicles. Studebaker featured popular personalities to tell their story while Oldsmobile sought to promote better gas mileage. Dodge's fluid drive ads invited potential customers to visit car lots for tryout drives. Packard utilized its long sweeping body to fill an entire page of advertisement. All companies joined Nash's emphasis, "At last, something new in the lowest-priced field." It was smart to buy a car in 1941 because this was the last year new cars would be available until after the end of World War II.

DeSoto Deluxe Six-Passenger Sedan

REPRINTED WITH PERMISSION FROM CHRYSLER GROUP LLC

Nash Ambassador

REPRINTED WITH PERMISSION FROM CHRYSLER GROUP LLC

Oldsmobile

REPRINTED WITH PERMISSION FROM GENERAL MOTORS COMPANY

REPRINTED WITH PERMISSION OF STUDEBAKER NATIONAL MUSEUM

Packard Custom Convertible Victoria

The Metro Daily News

FINAL EDITION

JANUARY 20, 1941

FRANKLIN D. ROOSEVELT INAUGURATED FOR THIRD TERM AS PRESIDENT OF THE UNITED STATES

Franklin D. Roosevelt is the only president to be elected for three terms.

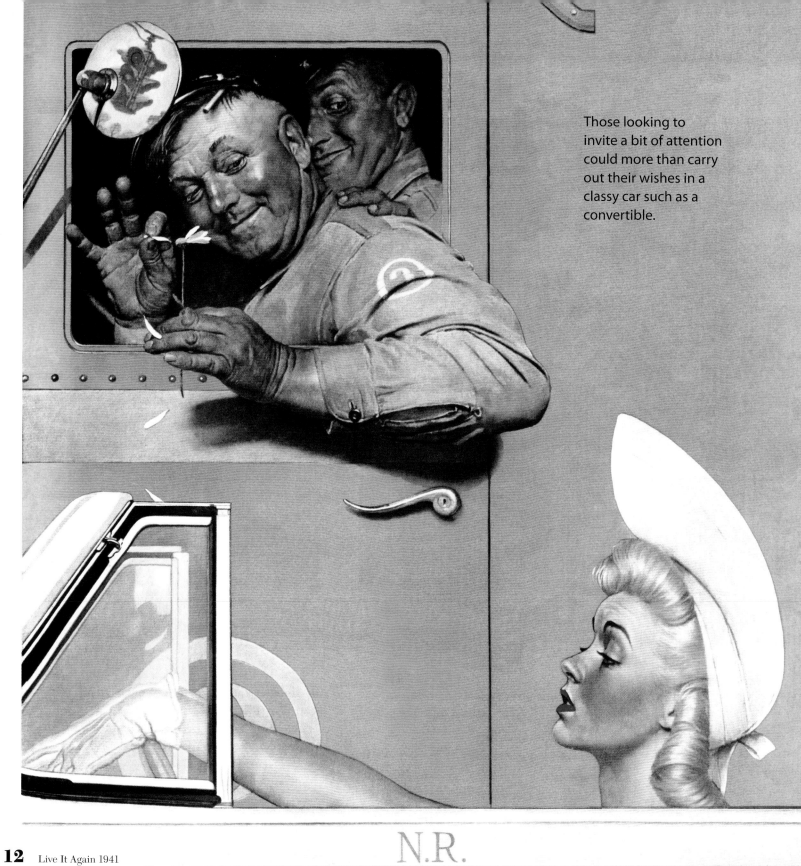

Those looking to invite a bit of attention could more than carry out their wishes in a classy car such as a convertible.

Cars of 1941

Making a purchase

Purchasing a car in 1941 had a totally personal approach, especially in smaller towns. Shopping for a car was often a family experience, with the entire gang visiting the dealer to try out a brand-new vehicle. In neighborhood communities, it wasn't unusual for dealers to offer cars on a trial basis for several days, especially over a weekend.

Once the style of the car was determined, the customer would decide which extra accessories to add to the order. The car was then ordered by the dealer and delivered from the factory directly to the dealership, tailor-made for the customer.

REPRINTED WITH PERMISSION FROM FORD MOTOR COMPANY

REPRINTED WITH PERMISSION OF GULF PRIDE OIL

Purchasing a brand-new car was quite the thrill especially for first-time buyers. Just sitting in the driver's seat feeling the new upholstery could encourage a purchase.

RTESY OF THE DOW CHEMICAL COMPANY

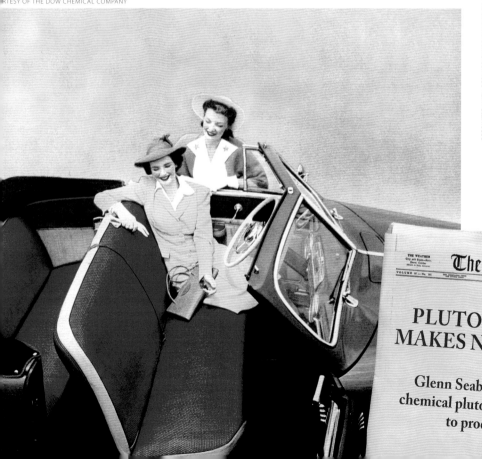

THE WEATHER
City and State—Rain; Snow; Colder

The Metro Daily News

FINAL EDITION

VOLUME 97 — No. 181

25 PAGES   FIVE CENTS

FEBRUARY 23, 1941

PLUTONIUM DISCOVERY MAKES NUCLEAR WEAPONS POSSIBLE

Glenn Seaborg and his team identify the chemical plutonium, which makes it possible to produce the atomic bomb.

© LIBRARY OF CONGRESS, PRINTS AND PHOTOGRAPHS DIVISION, CPH 3F05436

President Franklin D. Roosevelt

Leading the nation

On Jan. 20, 1941, Franklin D. Roosevelt made history when he was sworn in as the country's first three-term president. During the campaign, he stressed his extensive experience and bold leadership during the Great Depression. By year's end, Roosevelt would muster those attributes in the aftermath of Pearl Harbor.

Roosevelt's major foreign policy initiatives included the Lend-Lease Act—outlined on Jan. 6 in his famous "Four Freedoms" speech to Congress—which ended the semblance of neutrality. Through the act, Congress initially authorized $1.3 billion to furnish its allies with food, machinery and military equipment. Domestically, the growth of defense spending expanded the economy. The labor shortage in northern industrial cities led to an exodus from rural America. The number of unemployed dropped below 1 million.

The unthinkable happened when the Japanese navy attacked Pearl Harbor. Roosevelt's stirring oratory on Dec. 8 before a joint session of Congress lifted the country's spirits, when he vowed, "No matter how long it may take us to overcome this premeditated invasion, the American people in their righteous might will win through to absolute victory."

The Roosevelts celebrate Easter Sunday. In her syndicated column, Eleanor Roosevelt remarked about an uncertain future for the young. "I pray that we, who are older, may be able to help them during this difficult time."

President Roosevelt acknowledged the crowd after being sworn in by Chief Justice Charles Evan Hughes Sr. He declared in his inaugural address that, "our strong purpose is to protect and to perpetuate the integrity of democracy."

On May 1, President Roosevelt bought the first U.S. government Defense Savings Bond from Treasury Secretary Henry Morganthau Jr. When the war ended in 1945, a total of $185.7 billion of securities had been sold.

What Made Us Laugh

"Could I take it inside and look at it in the artificial light?"

"Larson, how many times must I tell you that any news you hear over the radio isn't a scoop?"

"Something to compete with a uniform."

"As near as I can make out, this guy is a novelist— and he doesn't want any milk this morning."

"We don't actually have a radio in every room, sir, but I can put you in 633—and there's a radio in 608 which can be heard anywhere on the floor, our guests assure us."

"There must be some mistake. He said 'Cordially' at the end of a letter to the Bureau of Internal Revenue."

"… And how long overdue do you let a bill run before you send a collector around?"

"The prices you guys charge, I don't blame you for wearing masks!"

The country general store served rural areas with a large variety of merchandise which included gasoline, groceries, repair accessories and various hardware items.

In the Neighborhood

Where we shopped

Neighborhood communities were still self-sufficient with Main Street businesses that took care of most of the family's needs. Clothing stores, groceries, dime stores and shoe stores were available within a short distance from the residential area.

Stores offered neighborhood-friendly service to local residents. Opportunities were there for local employment. Clerks knew patrons on a personal basis, including clothing sizes and grocery needs. The shopping experience for many people often turned into a social gathering.

"We tried to give it a homey, lifelike touch, Boss!"

Some men's clothing stores were more sophisticated than others, offering a full line of shirts, shoes and suits to allow a man to look his very best.

1941 ARMSTRONG CORK COMPANY

The local bakery offered irresistible fresh-baked items every morning. It was a favorite spot to pick up special cakes, pies, doughnuts and cookies.

Many Main Street businesses were owned by the same family for several generations. Loyal town residents supported and shopped at the local stores.

Service-station attendants would check the oil in vehicles, clean windshields and even wipe off mirrors as a part of regular customer service.

FAMOUS BIRTHDAYS

Nick Nolte, February 8 actor

Buffy Sainte-Marie, February 20 singer

Gasoline was personally pumped by friendly employees as part of the courtesy of business practices.

JULY SERVICE TIP

Vacation soon? Drive in for Shell-ubrication—a "Thoro-Fast" service that puts the right lubricant in the right spots in the right amount.

In the Neighborhood

Service with a smile

The personable touch of the neighborhood spirit was evident in business contacts and those serving community residents.

From the doctor's office to the local grocery store, each business knew the needs of the customer. A sense of trust existed between them by allowing patrons to charge for their purchased goods. Store owners competed in providing services to customers, often reaching out to families with candy for children or gifts on special occasions. Those caring for utility needs knew their recipients on a first-name basis and often took time for a friendly chat.

REPRINTED WITH PERMISSION FROM HEINZ

REPRINTED WITH PERMISSION OF PRUDENTIAL FINANCIAL, INC.

Mailmen knew those on their routes on a personal basis. They were also aware of the habits of those to whom they delivered mail; quite often, if things seemed out of routine, they would do a quick check during delivery, especially at homes of the elderly.

City Life

Out on the town

Life in the city was still filled with elegance and glamour for many people. Ladies wore glamorous silk or satin evening gowns, always with gloves; men wore tuxedos, sometimes with white tie and tails.

Dinner dates were not casual affairs either. Ladies wore hats, suits or nice dresses, and men wore suits or sport coats (or as the year progressed, military uniforms).

Formal manners were very much in vogue with men holding doors and chairs for ladies and standing when a lady came into the room.

From elegant cocktail parties to dinner dates at fancy restaurants, couples (even young couples just starting out!) would dress up in their best evening wear, or hats and suits for a night on the town.

For most of 1941, the United States was at peace, so city lights across the country still burned bright night and day.

Men going out for the evening still wore tuxedos, but sometimes they needed a little help from a willing female with those pesky bow ties!

JOHN HYDE PHILLIPS

The Metro Daily News

FINAL EDITION

MARCH 17, 1941

NATIONAL GALLERY OF ART OPENS IN WASHINGTON, D.C.

President Roosevelt accepts the completed building and art collections on the behalf of the American people at an evening ceremony.

Swimming and sunbathing along Lake Michigan was a way Chicagoans relaxed and cooled off on sweltering summer days when the city wasn't quite so windy.

Chicago's 3.4 million residents typically lived in cramped quarters among the city's many brownstone and gray stone-lined neighborhoo᷍ In 1941, Chicago was the second most populou᷍ city in the United States behind New York.

In 1941, Chicago continued construction on its first subway system. Below the hectic streets and massive towers, thousands of workers pushed through 8¾ miles of stiff clay before the first lines opened in 1943.

The Belt Railway Clearing Yards spanned 786 acres, supporting over 250 miles of track. It was a symbol of Chicago's position as a transcontinental crossroad for freight and commerce.

The Windy City

Chicago

Carl Sandburg's 1916 poem *Chicago* defined this great city's roots: "Hog Butcher for the World,/ Tool Maker, Stacker of Wheat,/ Player with Railroads and the Nation's Freight Handler:/ Stormy, husky, brawling,/ City of the Big Shoulders:." In 1941, Chicago was the bustling crossroad between East and West, North and South. From the boardrooms of its grand skyscrapers to the frenzied floors of its commodities exchanges to its vast stockyards, rail yards and lakeside docks, Chicago was a hub of commerce, industry, agriculture and freight.

Chicago was also a cultural and architectural center. "The Chicago School" of design and building was exported to the world. The musical sounds of Chicago included hot jazz, down-home blues, and sacred gospels. Its universities led the way in science, technology, art and literature. Its pro sports teams thrilled crowds at Wrigley Field, Comiskey Park and Chicago Stadium.

Chicago in 1941 was a tightly knit and inspiring home to millions of people of different races, faiths and cultures.

Chicago's Magnificent Mile includes the Water Tower (foreground) and Palmolive Building. The 37-story art deco-inspired Palmolive Building included a beacon that guided planes to Midway Airport.

The Great Migration of tens of thousands of Southerners to Chicago included blues and jazz musicians such as Lonnie Johnson (standing, left). They heated up the clubs along "The Stroll," the South Side's economic and entertainment district.

Showing your girl how to use something—a guitar, a gun, even a sextant—was a surefire way to get close to her (and everyone knows that girls love a man in uniform!)

THE SATURDAY EVENING POST

An

Found

VOLUME 213, NUMBER 32

Feb. 8, 1941

5c.

M°CLELLAND BARCLAY

Love and Courtship

While many men had begun to enlist in the armed services in anticipation of war, large numbers of men were still in school and working; therefore, courtships and dating were still taking place at a normal, leisurely pace.

Couples enjoyed dinner and movie dates, drives in the country or nights out on the town. School dances and sporting events kept most young couples entertained on the weekends. Parents usually had curfews for their teenagers, and they liked to meet their daughters' dates (ask any grown man, and he probably remembers this ordeal).

Even the rich and upper crust craved a burger at a coffee shop after a night on the town.

metimes parents liked to send a little brother or sister along on tes as a chaperone, especially if the date was a moonlight picnic.

An afternoon drive in a luxurious convertible was a great date.

Full skirts with crinolines underneath were a very popular silhouette for bridal gowns in 1941, inspired by the full skirt of Scarlett O'Hara's dresses in the 1939 motion picture, *Gone with the Wind*.

FAMOUS BIRTHDAYS
John Aprea, March 4 actor

Beautiful Brides

In 1941, lucky brides could still plan their dream weddings. Until Dec. 7, life in the United States went on as usual with no fabric shortages or gas rationing to restrict brides' choices.

Gowns were still made of satin and silk, with yards of fabric billowing out into full skirts or long trains. Grooms wore formal suits, tuxedos or morning suits, depending on the formality of the wedding. After the wedding, many couples were able to take honeymoon trips before setting up housekeeping.

In the prewar months of 1941, sumptuous silks and satins were still available to make the elegant bridal gowns that every girl dreamed about for her wedding day.

Fathers enjoyed their last moments with their daughters before going to the church and officially "giving them away."

Very formal weddings called for morning suits, top hats and gloves for the groom.

"Please, Arthur! My make-up!"

1941 was the last year until the war was over for most couples to enjoy the luxury of a formal wedding and a honeymoon trip.

Precious Smiles

Peacetime reigned for most of the year, and kids could just be kids. The economy had improved, and families were living with fewer money concerns, so they had the time and the energy to enjoy family time.

Little girls looked precious in their little dresses, ribbons and pinafores, and little boys still wore short pants. No matter how many years go by, parents can always look back and remember their children's precious smiles, so innocent and sweet!

Moms loved to do their little girls' hair in the popular "Shirley Temple curls" style.

FAMOUS BIRTHDAYS
Peggy Lennon, April 8 singer
Ann-Margret, April 28 Swedish-born actress

From newborns to toddlers, there was nothing like a child's smile to light up the day.

le girls in pinafores
ked sweet as pie!

Children could still wave
goodbye to Daddy as he
went off to work in those
heady prewar days.

Preparations are being made for a family outing as Mom packs the picnic basket.

THE WEATHER
City and State—Rain,
Snow, Colder
Shower in Early Afternoon

The Metro Daily News

FINAL EDITION

VOLUME 97 — No. 184 — 22 PAGES — FIVE CENTS

APRIL 6, 1941

GERMANY INVADES YUGOSLAVIA AND GREECE

Hitler tries to secure countries on his southern flank in anticipation of his invasion of the Soviet Union.

Family Time

Spending time together was the most important dynamic of family life in 1941. A closeness that had developed in toughing it out through the Great Depression continued with teamwork in most activities.

Much of the time spent together centered on playing or inventing games in the family backyard. Inside, cooking meals, dining as a family and playing board games all provided time to enjoy and laugh with other family members.

Neighborhood life provided community closeness. School activities, church programs, social clubs and carnivals all played their part in supplying memory-making opportunities.

© 1941 SEPS

Jumping on Dad for a friendly wrestle provided good interaction and competitive fun between family members.

A more formal dress code was mandatory in many households for Sunday noon meals as well as dinner during the week.

In encapsulating the many moods of childhood, Hunter understood what made children grin and cringe, as well as what would put a smile on a reader's face.

Post Covers by
Frances Tipton Hunter

She may not have achieved the notoriety afforded to her male contemporaries, but it is undeniable that Frances Tipton Hunter illustrated some of the more memorable *Saturday Evening Post* covers. Beginning with her June 6, 1936, cover "No Money for Her Soda," Hunter's flair was detailing the nation's notions of childhood, capturing the subtle facial expressions and body language around broad subjects.

Born in 1896, Hunter lost her mother at age 6, and grew up with an aunt and uncle in Williamsport, Pa. After graduating with honors from one of Philadelphia's top art schools, Hunter settled in New York City, finding work illustrating fashion layouts. Prior to her first *Post* cover, Hunter produced covers for national magazines such as *Collier's* and created a successful line of paper dolls.

Hunter illustrated 18 *Post* covers through the late 1940s, elevating her to one of the top female illustrators of her time.

© 1941 SEPS

© 1941 SEPS

Goodyear's Pliofilm was a flexible, durable and transparent rubber sheet that could be used to make raincoats and package foods.

GIVE THESE GAY NEW
Pliofilm
"USEFULS"

THE GOODYEAR TIRE & RUBBER COMPANY

1941 B.F. GOODRICH

We don't know a better way to tell you that

Koroseal is *Waterproof*

B.F. Goodrich's Koroseal was a compound made from coke, limestone and salt. When applied to fabric, it made the material sunproof, waterproof, washable and odorless.

1941 LEAD INDUSTRIES ASSOCIATION

Lead-based paint made sense in 1941—it was quick drying and resilient. Decades later, scientists discovered how toxic lead paint was to humans, particularly children under age 6.

FAMOUS BIRTHDAYS
Bobby Cox, May 21 baseball manager
Bob Dylan, May 24 poet and musician

Manufacturing

Making life easier

The military and industry greatly benefited from the creation of polymers and man-made rubbers, but so did all citizens. These pliable polymers and rubber substitutes could be found in a variety of products, from car tires and shower curtains to raincoats and evening gowns.

Items treated with these man-made materials were advertised as making consumer goods and textiles durable, water resistant and impervious to sun damage. Another benefit was that materials treated with these new additives were easy to clean. Dust and stains on coats, bags, swimsuits and gowns could be wiped away with a damp cloth, or washed without fear of immediate deterioration and erosion.

Nylon—a silk substitute—gave legs a luxurious sheen, but the man-made material was also used in parachutes and flak jackets.

1941 Style

Home decor

The average American probably didn't give much thought to home furnishings during the Great Depression, so, in 1941 when the economy started to recover, they were ready to redecorate!

Modern furniture with clean lines was becoming popular, but traditional styles were still preferred in many homes. Floral patterns, stripes and plaids were widely used in living rooms and bedrooms in brighter colors.

For kitchens, brightly patterned linoleum floors and bright accent colors were on the "wish list," but appliances were still usually white or stainless steel. The clean-and-tidy look was definitely popular in 1941.

This fashionable living room featured floral fabrics, offset by stripes, in the reds and greens that were popular with designers. The red whole-room carpet would have been a luxury back in 1941.

The average home was smaller in 1941 than what we're accustomed to today, so space was always at a premium. A bedroom set like this one would have been a real space saver with its practical headboard, featuring extra drawers and bookshelves.

The lucky lady who had this kitchen would have been the envy of the neighborhood! The bright linoleum floor, modern cabinets and the built-in banquette were state of the art in 1941.

White sinks, toilets and tubs were the standard, giving the bathroom a clean, fresh look.

The Metro Daily News

FINAL EDITION

THE WEATHER
City and Suburbs
Snow, Colder

FIVE CENTS

VOLUME 63 — No. 121

MAY 6, 1941

BOB HOPE PERFORMS HIS FIRST USO SHOW

Hope and a group of celebrities perform for airmen stationed at March Field in California.

Innovations in cooking included ovens with "look-in doors" and oven lights that let you see your food as it cooked.

Electric refrigerator/freezers were improving all the time, and you could buy a brand-new model for between two and three hundred dollars.

New lighter-weight irons featured steam, a "new convenience." They also promised women "no more wrist aches from lifting and tilting heavy, old-fashioned irons.

STEAM, TOO!

New Proctor *Never-Lift* lets you iron
with or without steam . . no lifting . . no drudgery

1941 Style

Modern appliances

Modern appliances were beginning to make life easier and save people time. Most metals were still being used to manufacture items for consumers instead of equipment needed for the war, so people could go out and buy the new conveniences.

Manufacturers advertised to women, promising to save them from drudgery and to give them more time to do other things. And the truth was that the new small appliances were taking many labor-intensive steps out of everyday housework.

Waffle Bakers, automatic toasters, mixers, coffee makers and the like were luxuries for the kitchen, and they were much-anticipated wedding gifts.

1941 SUNBEAM PRODUCTS

There were so many appliances to choose from—everything from "waffle bakers" and automatic toasters to mixers and coffee makers.

Women were excited to see washing machines that allowed them to simply put the clothes in, turn a dial and add soap … and it shut itself off when the load was done!

What Made Us Laugh

"Why not bring that biscuit dough in here?
My feet aren't doing anything."

"I don't have to plan my vacation. My boss tells
me when to go, and my wife tells me where."

"You and your midnight snacks in bed!"

"No, thanks, I'm just resisting."

"You think this is bad? Wait till
we get a two-ocean Navy."

"Every time I see Mickey Rooney it takes me a
week to get used to Richard again."

"Wasn't that ending used in another picture recently?"

"I'm quite positive he still loves you,
Miss. I distinctly heard him reply three
times in the affirmative."

THE *New* INTERNATIONAL

International Harvester made trucks which were geared for powerful, rugged travel in adverse weather and geographical situations.

International Harvester trucks were constructed to haul products in every type of situation on the road and for months of grueling punishment.

White Motor Co. produced heavy trucks to work such projects as the Ravenna Ordnance Arsenal in Ohio.

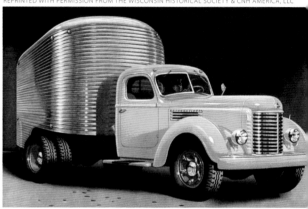

The K-Line International Harvester trucks were produced for use in national defense. Their Hi-Tork brakes were made for smooth straight-line stops. Coupled with easier steering, they were advertised for their safety in the midst of quick, braking speed changes.

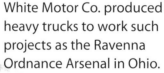

The Metro Daily News

FINAL EDITION

JUNE 14, 1941

GERMAN AND ITALIAN ASSETS IN THE UNITED STATES ARE FROZEN

President Roosevelt issues an executive order to freeze assets of Axis powers.

Trucks

Competition in truck sales centered around smoother riding vehicles, road care and greater safety. International Harvester advertised vehicles that had smooth breaks, easier steering for safer travel and hydraulic brakes to guide straight-line stops. Safety glass was being manufactured and introduced into vehicles. Trucks were streamlined for less resistance in long road travel.

More ability to climb steep grades with full loads was on the agenda to increase Ford sales. The increased power was also geared toward giving trucks higher speeds on open roads and faster acceleration in city traffic.

As truck sales increased and used a variety of new products, there was a trickle-down effect in the need for suppliers which increased the labor force and gave another boost to the strengthening economy.

This K-Line International was especially made to give greater fuel economy. Its safety comfort cab was considered to give greater performance for those riding in the cab and for navigation of the vehicle.

Ford pickups were promoted to move heavy loads more easily and to maintain sustained speeds in open-road driving.

Ford truck dealers offered on-the-job testing to accommodate cost and performance for wartime use.

Country Life

From earliest memories, children raised in the country learned to love animals, work hard and enjoy their natural surroundings. There was plenty to do and fun to be enjoyed—from riding the family horse to playing a game of hide-and-seek. Many lessons of life were taught through nature around them.

The cozy setting of the farm encouraged family members to work together during chores, when preparing meals and in times of need. When other families experienced difficulties, the farming neighborhood pulled together to assist them.

© 1941 SEPS

The Sept. 13, 1941, *Post* cover featured Man o' War at age 24, who was an all-time racing champion. Man o' War is nuzzling William Harbut, his groom since 1930.

"I'm new here—what are we supposed to do now?"

Family chickens sometimes gave special greetings to the mailman.

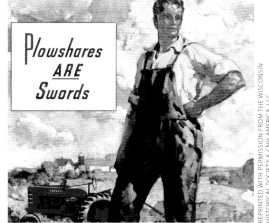

Plowshares ARE Swords

Various posters of the time upheld the importance of the farmer's hard work to provide for the nation's welfare.

Riding horses while Father farmed the field was a special way of family connection during times of hard work.

Lloyd Shaw and his Cheyenne Mountain Dance School trained teachers and teams of dancers, bringing the joy of square dancing to people across the country, making it popular in small towns and cities alike.

FAMOUS BIRTHDAYS
Myron Scholes, July 1 economist, Nobel prize laureate
Paul Anka, July 30 Canadian-American singer and songwriter

Young people enjoyed the fast pace of square dancing, and dances were a popular place to meet with friends on the weekends.

Country Life

Entertainment

Many Americans lived in rural areas in 1941, and though far from the lights and bustle of the big cities, they still found many ways to entertain themselves.

Square dancing had long been popular in the country, and it enjoyed a revival that spread across the country in 1941. From barns to church halls, the familiar ring of the callers rang out.

Church functions, like box-supper auctions, were also a big part of community entertainment. School events, especially sporting events, would often draw huge crowds on the weekends.

Leisurely pursuits like hunting and fishing were also very popular ways to spend a day.

© 1941 SEPS

Young people always found ways to enjoy time together, whether it was rounding up money for a box-supper auction or a leisurely day spent quietly fishing.

A 29-hour journey in a Pullman car from Chicago to Miami was a trip that combined the best style and service.

Vacation Destinations

In the face of an uncertain future and tightening of purse strings, a vacation was a chance to enjoy life. The peak season was June through August, but a winter jaunt was a way to reenergize. Vacation was a chance to reconnect with family and friends. However, couples and families took the time to tour the country's great cities of the time: New York, Boston, Washington, Chicago, Miami and San Francisco. Big cities offered the most activities, from museums and historical landmarks to shopping and fine dining.

A road trip by car was common. Over 3 million people traveled by plane in 1941, but flying was still considered exotic. A trip by train—roomy, romantic and practical—was the way to go. Bus terminals were also filled with tourists.

"No, no, madam. You don't stick the gum in your ears to relieve the air pressure. You chew it!"

For a young couple, the bus was an economical way to visit far-flung destinations from Florida to California.

Car ownership redefined mobility, as it opened up spontaneous travel like a weekend getaway to the shore.

Piper aircraft made plane ownership nearly as easy to do as buying a car.

Lifetime memories were made on vacation such as the breathtaking view on the Golden Gate Bridge.

The Metro Daily News

THE WEATHER
City and State—Rain,
Snow, Colder

VOLUME 80 — No. 181

FINAL EDITION

70 PAGES   FIVE CENTS

AUGUST 1, 1941

1ST JEEP ROLLS OFF THE ASSEMBLY LINE

The first mass-produced Jeep for the U.S. Army is manufactured in Toledo, Ohio.

For the young, going to the beach was a chance to show off well-toned physiques and the latest summer fashions.

The beach was more than just swimming. Boating was a good way to have fun and relax on a summer day.

A family going to the beach would pack a basket of good food from home. It saved money and time.

Fishing along a quiet stretch of beach was an ideal way to spend idle time.

Summer Fun

A day at the beach

When the asphalt got hot enough to fry an egg, a public beach was the place to cool down. The dog days of summer could be quickly shed by packing up the children, filling a picnic basket and finding the giant umbrella and beach ball. The fun could begin—as soon as a spot on the sand could be claimed. Typical activities were water sports, sunbathing and ball games. At night, people would warm themselves by making a fire of driftwood.

Not all beaches were the same. The ideal experience was chronicled in the July 5, 1941 edition of the *Post*, when New York's Jones Beach was highlighted as the ideal getaway. Unlike crowded Coney Island, writer Edmond Fish described Jones Beach as an oasis of good taste. "Flowers, lawns, shrubs greet you," he wrote. "Nothing is crowded … The beach is apparently endless."

Fun and Frolic

Many boys learned how to play baseball emulating their heroes on sandlot fields.

A child's life was simple, but no less fun and imaginative. A backyard was the Wild West, a sandlot doubled as Yankee stadium, and a boat race could take place in a rain gutter. A dollhouse was really the fabulous home of a radiant Hollywood starlet.

Kids prided themselves in their expertise at shooting marbles or being impossible to find when playing hide-and-seek. It was also a do-it-yourself age. A rusty can was recycled for a game of Kick the Can, and an old clothesline would do for jumping rope.

When the days were hot, children became entrepreneurs, opening lemonade stands. In winter, a sled and a hill were a good way to play, followed by some hot cocoa to warm up.

...mmer fun included a beach pail and ...ovel to mold sand creations.

...resh-squeezed lemonade on a ...ot day was a treat for kids and a ...vay to make some money.

The Metro Daily News

THE WEATHER
City and State—Mild
Sun. Colder
...

VOLUME 37 — No. 184

FINAL EDITION

10 PAGES   FIVE CENTS

SEPTEMBER 27, 1941

"BLUE CHAMPAGNE," PERFORMED BY JIMMY DORSEY, IS NO. 1 ON THE MUSIC CHARTS

Jimmy Dorsey had 12 Top-10 hits in 1941.

What Made Us Laugh

"We wished on the moon. ... It was so romantic. ...
Then he tells me he wished for two new front tires."

"George is looking for ants carrying crumbs. Then he
takes the crumbs away from them just for spite."

"Fortunately, we've been spared our chauffeur.
The Draft Board rejected him for bad eyesight!"

"I get off next. My phone number is
Crestview 8942. Will you call me when
you find out who done it?"

"You think I'm terrible, Mom thinks I'm terrible, Pop thinks I'm terrible, and I know I'm terrible, so what's the use of going on?"

"Not yet, Marvin. Let him come in! I've been trying to get that window open for a year!"

"I send my homework to Information Please. If they can't do it you get twenty-five bucks."

"Look—he even hasn't got hair like his father hasn't!"

Making homemade ice cream was often a memorable experience for grandchildren on a hot summer day.

There was nothing like a warm bowl of Grandma's soup for a grandson who was serving in the military and home on leave.

Everyday Life

Grandparents are special

Back in 1941 many grandchildren were blessed by living close to their grandparents. The presence of grandparents added a dimension of help, wisdom and love to the family. Trips to grandparents' house were a favorite for grandchildren. Granddaughters bonded with their grandmothers while baking goodies, and grandsons often enjoyed creating wood projects with their grandpas.

The value of well-seasoned wisdom was often an asset to parents who appreciated a bit of advice in child rearing from time to time. Bedtime stories read or told by grandparents often became the highlight of the day for family members.

Grandchildren loved to sit on Grandpa's lap and ask questions about what life was like when he was their age.

There were plenty of fishing lessons available with Grandpa's guidance at the pond.

Beauty Rarin' to Go!

Horses used for show or leisure enjoyment became special friends to owners and family members.

THE SATURDAY EVENING POST
5cts. 7c. IN CANADA · Nov. L'41

GOSH, BILL! WISH I HAD A DOG LIKE YOURS!

THE SATURDAY EVENING POST
An Founded
Dec. 6, 1941
VOLUME 214, NUMBER 23
5cts.
7c. IN CANADA

All cares faded away when children looked into the loving eyes of their pets.

The Animals
We Loved

From early on, animals have taught us lessons in love and care. Children were taught responsibilities through caring for their pets. Naming animals aided in the bonding process between a favorite pet and the entire family.

For children and the elderly, horses, dogs, cats and even birds and fish provided a special sense of companionship. Some animals, such as horses and farm pets, taught valuable lessons through 4-H projects. The elderly found a special friend to talk to with their family pet. Children also utilized their friendships with animals to talk over some of the problems they experienced with friends and school.

REPRINTED WITH PERMISSION OF UNITED STATES STEEL CORPORATION

A good walk with the dog was always a great way to exercise.

1941 INTERNATIONAL SILVER CO.

© 1941 SEPS

BEGINNING **THE MURDER OF THE FIFTH COLUMNIST** By LESLIE FORD

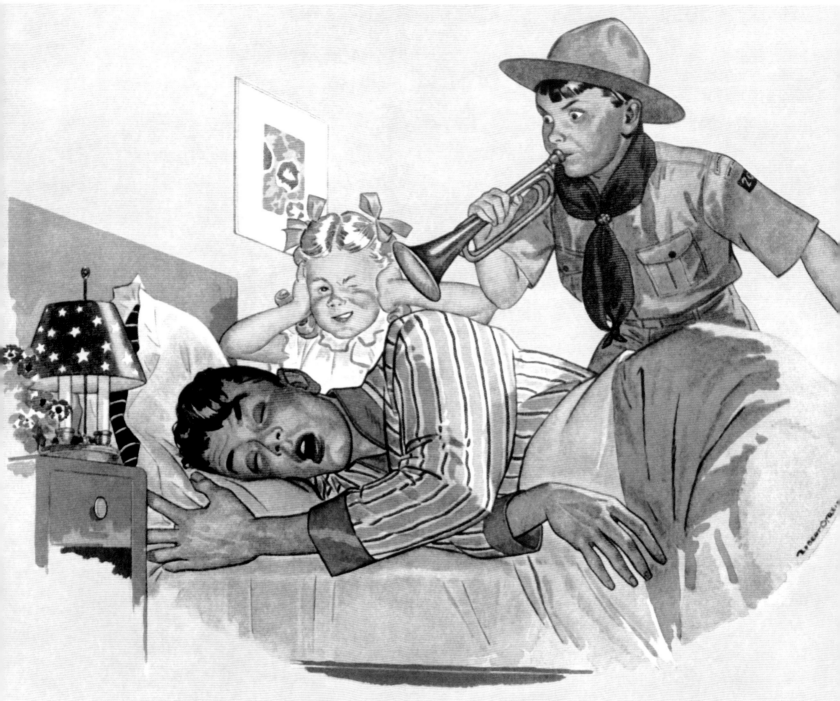

Activities such as scouting often provided tempting opportunities to unleash stored-up energy into creative pranks. This dad just wanted to get in some extra needed sleep which he obviously was unable to do.

Everyday Life

Mischief makers

Rubber bands and paper airplanes were among the weapons that were used by ornery children seeking to satisfy extra bursts of energy during long school days. Neighborhood club meetings would abound with stories of fun-filled pranks and retaliation among friends, sometimes aimed at role models such as teachers, parents and Sunday School teachers.

Often, the best way to channel the energy would be to create productive ways of harnessing its mischief. After-school chores, special projects and kind deeds toward others were all ways of turning orneriness into energy geared toward building positive self-esteem.

"Better humor her and play in the sandbox. We can work out that wing-load ratio after school."

1941 Style

The man about town

Suits were not just for businessmen in 1941. Men wore suits to church, to dinner and even to gatherings at friends' homes. Most men had at least one good suit in their closets.

Suit coats were single or double breasted, and men usually wore pocket squares. The shoulders were "accentuated" to enhance the popular, broad-shouldered silhouette. Trousers were full cut with "modified" high waists, front pleats and cuffs.

Hats were always worn with dress clothes when going out, and men knew the proper etiquette when wearing a hat. Hats were always removed indoors or when the national anthem played, and a tip of the hat was considered polite when saying hello or goodbye.

FAMOUS BIRTHDAYS

John Thompson, September 2
basketball coach
Dennis Ritchie, September 9
computer scientist

Shirt and tie were required in the white-collar workplace, and the sharp-dressed businessmen looked especially smart in a double-breasted suit with a pocket square.

Men didn't wear tennis shoes with their casual attire; instead, casual shoes ran the gamut from two-tone bluchers and thong-tied lounge shoes to woven oxfords.

The single-breasted suit was the standard for businessmen, with cuffed pants and well-shined dress oxfords. Suits were almost always worn to church, parties and dinners as well.

Suits and ties were not complete without a hat. Fedoras were an extremely popular and common style in 1941.

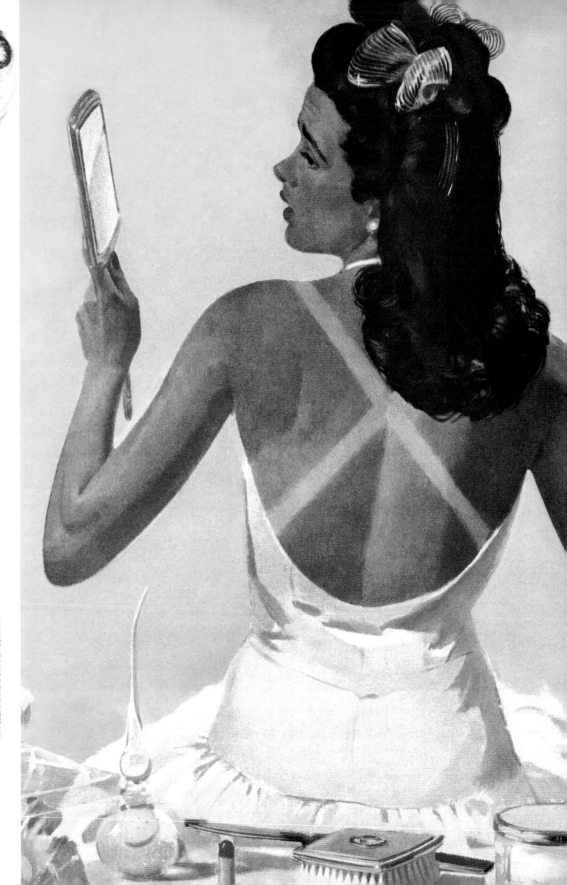

Many women didn't like
to leave home without
applying lipstick first—
and the bolder the red,
the better!

A hooded coat or cap was an elegant
way to protect a prized hair style, while
also achieving Hollywood glamour.

1941 Style

The fashionable lady

Personal grooming was considered to be very important for women in 1941. It showed pride and confidence in one's appearance. Lipstick was essential whenever one left home, and bare legs were not at all acceptable when dressing up.

All of this attention to appearances required quite a bit of time and effort. Hair had to be curled and rolled. Stockings required garter belts, and a girl might get an uncomfortable sunburn trying to get a little color (especially since there were no sunscreen products available!).

Before the war, women would not have considered going out without stockings; however, during the war, many women were forced to use leg makeup instead.

This young lady would have been considered very well put-together with her precisely groomed brows, perfectly applied red lipstick and carefully curled hair, finished with a pretty bow.

"When will I be old enough to wear the kind that kill you?"

1941 Style

Hats

Hats were *de rigueur* for women in 1941. Going out on the town, going to church—just about anywhere women went, they wore hats. It was a paradise for milliners, and the luckiest ladies had a closet filled with hat boxes since a well-made hat could be quite expensive.

Hats were often made of felt or straw for hot weather. Underneath, hair styles were usually shoulder length or a bit longer, and the hair was usually rolled or curled. Popular styles included fedoras, wide-brim hats, bonnets, berets and turbans. Ribbons, feathers (including ostrich feathers) and veils were used as accents.

A single feather served as a striking accent to a classic felt hat, and it added a touch of fun too.

A wide-brim hat, worn at a jaunty angle, could make a woman look oh-so-intriguing.

THE SATURDAY EVENING POST

An Illustrated Weekly
...un ...by Benj. Fr...

Oct. 11, 1941   5cts.
VOLUME 214, NUMBER 15   ...CANADA

A veiled hat added glamour and sophistication to an outfit, creating the kind of hat one usually saved for special occasions rather than everyday wear.

This hat, with its carefree tilt to the side, sports ostrich feathers, which were considered a "smart" way to accent a hat in 1941.

"You haven't all sorts of troubles you'll always be pouring out to me, have you?"

After dancing the night away, nothing felt quite as good as finally taking off your dancing shoes. A long dance could be quite exhausting!

Dances were a great place to meet that special someone, or the perfect date for steady couples. Despite the formal attire and atmosphere, young people still relaxed and enjoyed themselves.

Even young men sported the white tie tuxedo look when they went to a formal ball. As teenagers, they could finally appreciate those formal dance classes Mom made them take.

Entertainment

At the dance

When young people went to a dance in 1941, they actually danced! Kids loved to do the jitterbug, the jive, the Lindy Hop, and other dances to the sounds of the big bands. Glenn Miller, Tommy Dorsey, Duke Ellington and Benny Goodman ruled the music scene, and there wasn't any better music in the world for dancing the night away.

Ballroom dancing styles were also popular with everyone from kids to grandparents. People would waltz and do the fox trot, dressed in formal tuxedos and lovely full-length gowns. Grand ballrooms all over the country offered people a great place to meet, greet and enjoy a fun evening out.

A girl in a beautiful gown who was also a good dancer might have enjoyed spending the evening as the belle of the ball.

Glenn Miller's band performed three nights a week on a show sponsored by Chesterfield cigarettes. Miller's bassist credited the band's success to its leader: "Miller had America's musical pulse."

Entertainment

Radio days

A creaking door, the sinister tone of the narrator and creepy organ music highlighted the mystery anthology series *Inner Sanctum*, which debuted on Jan. 7, 1941. The show punctuated shocking tales of mayhem and murder with the morbid humor of its host Raymond Edward Johnson.

Top dramas were *Sherlock Holmes*, *The Shadow*, and *Captain Midnight*. America laughed at the antics of *Fibber McGee and Molly*, and its spin-off, *The Great Gildersleeve*. The swing era was in full effect. Glenn Miller, Cab Calloway, Duke Ellington and Tommy Dorsey set the tone from coast to coast.

Radio news' heyday was during this period. Some of the voices that brought the world to the home were Edward R. Murrow, Lowell Thomas, Walter Winchell and Dorothy Thompson.

"Next question: Give the first three letters of the alphabet—they don't have to be in their proper order."

The new General Electric FM console opened up a whole new world of radio, giving more powerful shortwave, finer domestic reception and FM—the new kind of broadcasting. With this FM feature, one could hear tones and overtones that the ordinary radio could not bring to the listener.

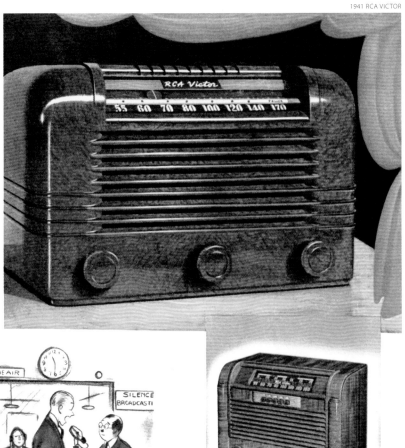

Radio Stars & Hits of 1941

Amos 'n' Andy

The Adventures of Ellery Queen

Bing Crosby

Captain Midnight

The Edgar Bergen and Charlie McCarthy Show

Fibber McGee and Molly

Glenn Miller Show

Inner Sanctum

Lights Out

Lone Ranger

The Shadow

The Adventures of the Thin Man

Tommy Dorsey Orchestra

"The opinions expressed on this program are those of the speaker's wife and do not necessarily represent the views of this station."

Portability and versatility were the theme of the day. RCA Victor had a radio or phonograph for every room and everybody. RCA Victor sold readers on its commitment to national defense and the value of its products. Fewer radios would be built, but "they will be finer than ever."

© BETTMANN/CORBIS

James Francis "Jimmy" Dorsey was one of the most popular bandleaders of the swing era. With singers Bob Eberly and Helen O'Connell, Dorsey used his signature three-section arrangement to spin a string of hits.

© BETTMANN/CORBIS

Saxophonist Freddy Martin and his band were radio regulars, but they also took the stage at prestigious hotels. Martin's biggest hit was 1941s "Piano Concerto in B Flat (Tonight We Love)," featuring Clyde Rogers on vocals.

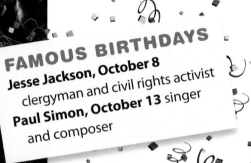

The Rainbow of Sound

REPRINTED WITH PERMISSION OF CROSLEY RADIO AND THE CROSLEY CORPORATION

Entertainment

Singers and big bands

The sound of 1941 was big-band swing. In a landscape featuring legendary bandleaders cranking out hits, it was Glenn Miller and Jimmy Dorsey who dominated the charts.

Miller finished the year with 11 Top-10 hits, including "Chattanooga Choo-Choo," which went No. 1 the week of Dec. 7. Jimmy Dorsey and his orchestra backed Bing Crosby and Frank Sinatra on radio. However, Dorsey's big hit was a redo of "Amapola (Pretty Little Poppy)," featuring Bob Eberly and Helen O'Connell on vocals. "Amapola" spent 10 weeks at the top of the Billboard pop chart.

Billie Holiday recorded "God Bless the Child" and Duke Ellington released "I've Got It Bad (And That Ain't Good)," both of which would become classic jazz standards for generations to come.

© BETTMANN/CORBIS

Top Hits of 1941

"Frenesi"
Artie Shaw

"Amapola (Pretty Little Poppy)"
Jimmy Dorsey

"Daddy"
Sammy Kaye

"Piano Concerto in B Flat" (Tonight We Love)
Freddy Martin

"Chattanooga Choo-Choo"
Glenn Miller

"Green Eyes (Aquellos Ojos Verdes)"
Jimmy Dorsey

"Maria Elena"
Jimmy Dorsey

"My Sister and I"
Jimmy Dorsey

"Song of the Volga Boatmen"
Glenn Miller

"Blue Champagne"
Jimmy Dorsey

"Elmer's Tune"
Glenn Miller

One of the finest clarinetists of all time, Artie Shaw was a swing-era genius. Although the pressure of early success caused him to briefly abandon music in 1939, Shaw quickly struck gold with his recording "Frenesi."

A precursor to the film-noir genre, *The Maltese Falcon* tells the story of private-eye Sam Spade and the unsavory characters involved in a mystery about murder and loot.

In *How Green Was My Valley*, Maureen O'Hara and Walter Pigeon were unforgettable in their central roles as an unmarried woman and a new minister in a Welsh mining town.

Entertainment

At the movies

The year 1941 was a memorable and controversial one in film history. Three legends released their masterpieces: Orson Welles' *Citizen Kane*, John Huston's *The Maltese Falcon* and John Ford's *How Green Was My Valley*. The latter—film adaptation of Richard Llewellyn's novel about a Welsh mining town—won the Best Picture Academy Award over the more critically acclaimed works by Welles and Huston.

Gary Cooper received accolades for his role as Sergeant York. Cooper's performance earned him his first Best Actor Oscar. The year's best films also included Alfred Hitchcock's suspense thriller *Suspicion*, Preston Sturges' comedy *Sullivan's Travels*, Walt Disney's *Dumbo* and the adaptation of Lillian Hellman's turn-of-the century Southern drama *The Little Foxes*.

Suspicion teamed Cary Grant and Joan Fontaine in a suspense thriller about quick courtship and fast betrayal. Fontaine won the Best Actress Academy Award.

Sergeant York is noted for its authentic portrayal of World War I's biggest hero. Cooper played Alvin York, a Tennessean who eventually single-handedly captured a large group of Germans.

Tops at the Box Office

Sergeant York

They Died With Their Boots On

Honky Tonk

A Yank in the RAF

How Green Was My Valley

Citizen Kane

Sullivan's Travels

Moon Over Miami

Buck Privates

Ziegfeld Girl

The Maltese Falcon

That Night in Rio

Meet John Doe

Suspicion

Children often helped Mom in the kitchen. Even in the most modern kitchen, there were many chores to do, from helping with the dishes and unloading groceries to taking out the trash and sweeping the floor.

After a long day of chores, school and playtime, nothing was better than a good book before bedtime.

1941 AMERICAN AIRLINES

1941 STEWART WARNER

In 1941, it was OK for children to sit in the front seat (and there were no safety belts!) when going out with Mom to run errands.

THE WEATHER
City and Suburbs—Fair.
Snow, Colder.

The Metro Daily News

FINAL EDITION

VOLUME 11—No. 194 · · FIVE CENTS

OCTOBER 23, 1941

WALT DISNEY'S *DUMBO* IS RELEASED

Goes on to win the Academy Award for Original Music Score

Everyday Life

Mother's little helper

The majority of mothers were at home, working in the house and caring for the children. New appliances had made some household chores easier, but many people still did not have electricity and did not own conveniences such as automatic washing machines.

Mothers usually expected children to do some chores around the house. Children growing up in the cities and small towns would help out with housework like dusting, washing dishes, sweeping and tidying their rooms, while children in rural areas helped around the house, in addition to helping with farm work and gardening.

After Pearl Harbor, many fathers enlisted in the Armed Forces, making it more important than ever before for children to help Mom out at home!

"There is an enduring tenderness in the love of a mother to a son that transcends all other affections of the heart."
—*Washington Irving*

"Durability isn't enough. I want a dress that will fight back."

Mothers and daughters always enjoyed a day of shopping together, taking in the sights and sounds of downtown, whether it was a small town or a big city.

Everyday Life

Fun with Father

"Daddy's home!" was a popular cry in the evening when fathers came home from a hard day at work.

Special things that fathers did with their children included flying kites, going fishing and repairing broken toys and other items around the house. Playing sports after dinner was always a family favorite.

Dads and children would often create games on the living room floor or take time to put together car and airplane models. Occasionally, there would be special "father and children only" group outings to sporting events, boating trips and other fun organized activities.

Sometimes it was fun to spend time at Dad's side pretending to be making the same thing Dad was working on.

1941 SERVEL INC.

REPRINTED WITH PERMISSION FROM GENERAL ELECTRIC COMPANY

Learning how to operate new purchases such as radios and record players was the assumed responsibility of fathers, who would then pass on understanding of the task to other family members.

THE SATURDAY EVENING POST

Weekly
Founded ... Benj. Franklin

5c.
7c. IN CANADA

August 30, 1941

VOLUME 214, NUMBER 9

Charles Dye

Driving boats or even small vehicles was a created moment that allowed children to feel "big" in their dad's arms. The guiding and guarding hand of Father was always right there.

Beginning

BIG FAMILY

By
BELLAMY PARTRIDGE

School girls in their sweaters, skirts and saddle oxfords, dreamed of being glamorous fashion models and cover girls.

Boys dreamed of being football heroes. Like the song says, "You gotta be a football hero to get along with a beautiful girl."

After graduation, many couples turned their though to serious relationships.

Everyday Life

School years

People often said that high school years were the best years of their lives … a time to be carefree and to have fun. 1941 may have been the last year that many girls and boys could enjoy those easy days because, after Dec. 7, their lives would change dramatically.

Until the United States entered the war, kids still enjoyed high school life. Football and basketball games were big events and were very well-attended. Boys and girls enjoyed the dating scene, with many people marrying someone they met and dated in school.

College kids enjoyed riding around in old jalopies and living it up at football games and campus parties. For most of 1941, school life was still a time to enjoy being young.

From quiet bike rides to double dates in crazy jalopies, boys and girls just wanted to be together, having a good time.

"Miss Thompson and Mr. Jackson! Have you forgotten this is a biology period?"

What Made Us Laugh

"Listen here, Hawkins, did you come to college to play football or to waste your time?"

"Sealed instructions from the owner—I'm not to open them till we're in the backstretch!"

"Personally, I'm for breaking this up. I feel too much like a defense poster."

THIS DRESSING ROOM FOR UMPIRES ONLY

E
XML
KJRAOPSTV
FGHNQROTS

"Who goes there? Name, address and
phone number."

"Is this geography test to be graded by the
early or late edition of the evening paper?"

"He's small. But I think you'll like him.
He can't count over ten, yet."

"Cut the speech short—we wanta get
started building the next ship."

On Oct. 4, 1927, work on Mount Rushmore began with a bang—dynamite was used to remove rock until a thin layer of granite was left. George Washington was completed on July 4, 1934, followed by Thomas Jefferson (1936), Abraham Lincoln (1937), and Theodore Roosevelt (1939). Construction was completed in October 1941.The project cost just under $1 million. Miraculously, despite the danger, there were no fatalities during carving.

United States Events

Domestically speaking, 1941 was a year of achievements and beginnings. The United Services Organizations—the USO—was founded in Times Square, New York in 1941. Six civilian agencies heeded President Franklin D. Roosevelt's call to provide recreation and increase morale for military personnel. The National Gallery of Art was dedicated on March 17, 1941. On May 1, CherriOats, later renamed Cherrios, were introduced to the public. Later that month, New York City Mayor Fiorello La Guardia was appointed first director of the Office of Civilian Defense.

Immigrants Margret and H.A. Rey published the first book in the *Curious George* series. After 14 years of work, Mount Rushmore was completed on Oct. 31. Its artist, Guston Borglum, died a few months earlier. And after much consternation among politicians and citizens, Congress officially made the fourth Thursday in November the national Thanksgiving Day. In 1939, Roosevelt had switched the holiday to the next-to-the-last Thursday of the month, giving merchants more time to sell during the Christmas season. Some states had followed the rule, others didn't.

During 1941, USO centers were established in nearly every imaginable place, from churches to beach clubs. Centers offered recreation, dances, movies, snacks and good cheer to soldiers far from home. Later, the USO shows would bring entertainment to the troops.

Americans rejoiced when Congress established the national Thanksgiving holiday to be celebrated on the fourth Thursday of November.

the National Gallery's dedication, President Roosevelt accepted the ilding and collection on behalf of the American people.

THE SATURDAY EVENING POST

An Illustrat...
Founded A° D! 172...

June 7, 1941

VOLUME 213, NUMBER 49

5cts.
7c. IN CANADA

BUILDER
No. 1

By
FRANK J.
TAYLOR

Everyday Life

Favorite pastimes

Favorite pastimes in 1941 included such simple pleasures as fishing, playing games around the table, enjoying music played on the upright piano or listening to stories on the old box radio.

Families enjoyed playing crochet or going to the local softball games. Even work such as gardening, canning fruit and taking flowers to the elderly brought neighbors and friends together. Ladies enjoyed quilting while sampling favorite candies and cookies.

Often on Sundays after church, families would gather for lunch and a good game of checkers. Adults would visit in their easy chairs while children played hide-and-seek and other creative games outside.

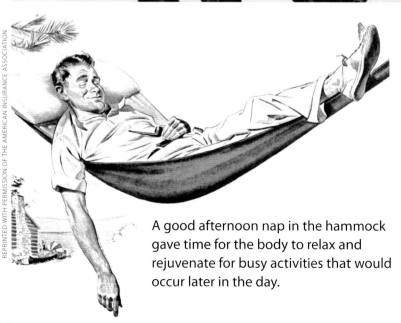

A good afternoon nap in the hammock gave time for the body to relax and rejuvenate for busy activities that would occur later in the day.

ENLARGING IS OUR SPECIALTY

After a day of hard work or play, sitting by a cozy fire was a comfortable way to relax for the evening.

Gardening was one of the favorite pastimes, both for pleasure and for food preparation for family eating. Gardeners sometimes liked to take breaks to read magazines filled with ideas for decorative flowerbeds.

"Nobody knew how to detach the darn thing."

"How will you have your 'No!'—with or without a slap in the face?"

"Charlie, do you still want to marry me?"

The work-a-day world wasn't easy, and one never knew what to expect!

Everyday Life

It's a living

Women were out in the workforce in 1941, but the jobs available to them were usually lower-paying jobs like waitressing, switchboard operators, store clerks or secretaries. White collar and professional jobs were rarely options for "working girls." Cartoons and magazine covers often portrayed women as fed up with work and dreaming of the ultimate goal—marriage and a family.

Sometimes life could be quite overwhelming for "the working girl," causing her to dream about marriage and children, or a more glamorous job.

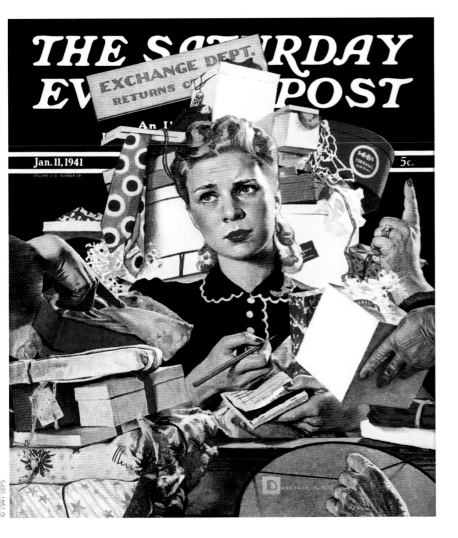

Sports and Recreation

Auto racing was coming into its own in 1941, while horse racing continued to maintain its popularity among major spectator sports. At Indianapolis, Floyd Davis and Mauri Rose teamed up for a race victory at the Indianapolis 500. At Churchill Downs, famed horse, Whirlaway, came through for another big-stakes victory, winning the Kentucky Derby.

A small amount of controversy followed Whirlaway's win due to the fact that it was thought the racehorse was in failing health earlier in the year. There were concerns the horse might have been given enhancing drugs, but tests proved those to be false. In recreational sports, games such as golf, bowling and tennis were becoming more popular for both men and women.

The May 30, 1941 Indianapolis 500 co-winners Floyd Davis and Mauri Rose won the race with the winning time of four hours, 20 minutes and 36.266 seconds. Their average speed per hour was 115.117. Rose relieved Davis during a pit stop after the car he started the race in had been pulled due to spark-plug problems.

Getting in a good game of golf became more popular for both men and women in 1941.

America's love for horse racing continued to grow as it brought together family and frien to cheer on their favorite horse, always hopi for a victory.

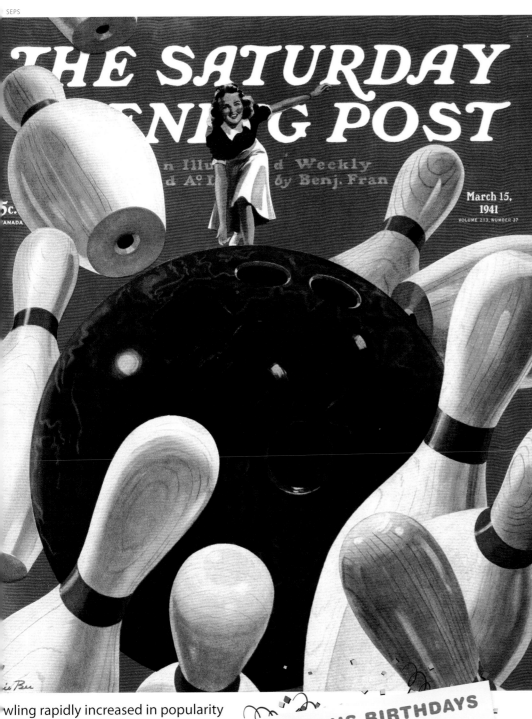

wling rapidly increased in popularity both men and women. Throughout e United States people joined bowling ubs at the neighborhood bowling ey where they could compete and ve fun with friends.

FAMOUS BIRTHDAYS

Art Garfunkel, November 5
singer
Bill Freehan, November 29
baseball player

Recreational tennis was a great way to exercise for both men and women. Competitive tennis for both men and women gained popularity as tennis tourneys grew in number.

Joe DiMaggio of the New York Yankees slammed out another hit in Washington, D.C., on June 29, 1941, part of a 56-game record-setting hitting streak.

Sports and Recreation

They were the champions

The New York Yankees had a big year in 1941, defeating the Brooklyn Dodgers 4-1 in the World Series. Team member Joe DiMaggio captured fans' hearts by hitting safely in 56 straight games and batting .406 for the season.

In professional football, the Chicago Bears lived up to their "Monsters of the Midway" status with a 37-9 defeat of the New York Giants to capture the National Football League championship.

The highlight of professional boxing occurred on June 18 when Joe Louis retained his title by knocking out Billy Conn with two seconds to go in round 13.

The Chicago Bears won their second straight National Football League championship at Wrigley Field with a win over the New York Giants.

Gene Pelham's painting of the great American football fan depicted the rigors of sitting in all kinds of weather to enjoy the game.

Billy Conn trained for his fight with Joe Louis for the World Heavyweight Championship. The encounter, which occurred in front of 54,487 fans at the Polo Grounds in New York City, was won by Louis in the 13th round.

Cute, yes, but scrap-metal recycling was a valuable service to the nation's defense buildup.

Patriotism

The spirit of 1941

In 1941, our nation met the inevitable specter of war in the air with a bold spirit of patriotism. Buying defense bonds was considered a practical and loyal thing to do—it was an investment in the nation's future. The government enlisted Hollywood stars to drive the sales effort. Magazines, print ads and billboards featured illustrations with patriotic symbols such as Uncle Sam, Old Glory, the Eagle and the Great Seal.

Even children got into the act, participating in scrap-metal drives that would help build America's defense. Enlistment in the military was on the rise. The Army alone had over 1 million recruits. Women sought to serve too. In May 1941, Congresswoman Edith Rogers introduced a bill to establish a Women's Army Auxiliary Corp.

To build public awareness of defense bonds, the government used creative spaces and places for its campaign. This giant photomural, designed by the Farm Security Administration, was installed in the concourse of New York City's Grand Central terminal. Composed of 22 photographs, the 85-foot mural was dedicated in December 1941.

It was common practice in 1941 to incorporate patriotic images on magazine cover illustrations and in corporate ad campaigns.

In a world of uncertainty, flags like these women are sewing were made for ships being built for the Navy and bought by fellow Americans who wanted to proudly display and affirm their love of country and its values.

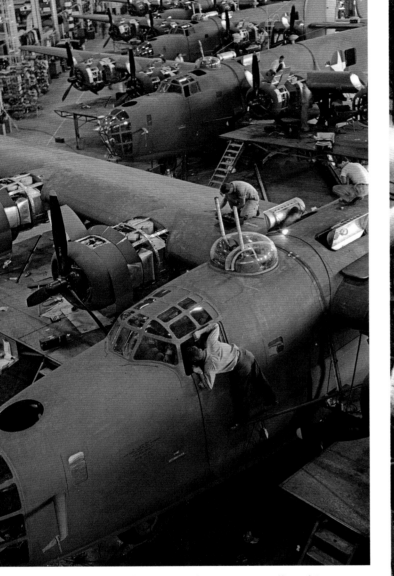

Seven months after its April 1941 groundbreaking, Ford's Willow Run, Mich., plant was ready for training. At its peak, the plant built 428 B-24's per month during the war.

Every industry had a job to do in the mobilization. Even seemingly insignificant peacetime products such as caster wheels were now valuable assets in the country's defense industry.

Preparing for War

Ramping up production

War mobilization was the business of America in 1941. Army procurement had grown from around a half billion dollars a year in 1939 to $26 billion in 1941. The Lend-Lease Act ended the pretense of neutrality. More of the United States' industrial capacity was devoted to meeting the military needs of the nation and its allies. Car companies, for example, retooled their plants nationwide to produce tanks, anti-aircraft guns, airplane parts and eventually airplanes.

Heat from the defense buildup also served as an incubator for innovation. In 1941, Chrysler's engineers were conceiving faster engines for planes. General Electric built the nation's first jet engine. RCA bought a tract of farmland outside Princeton, N.J., and created RCA Laboratories, which was instrumental in advancing game-changing technologies in RADAR, radio and anti-submarine warfare.

Introduced in 1941, the versatile and iconic Willys MB jeep would become, according to Gen. George C. Marshall, "America's greatest contribution to modern warfare."

More than just steel, warships were made from numerous raw materials. For example, rubber-related products—as small as seals to larger tools such as steam hoses and conveyer belts—were essential to shipbuilding.

© 1941 SEPS

THE SATURDAY EVENING POST

Feb. 1, 1941   5cts.

DRESS RIGHT
RIGHT FACE!
COUNT OFF!
PORT ARMS
LEFT ARMS
COLUMN RIGHT MARCH!
ABOUT FACE
RIGHT FACE
RIGHT SHOULDER ARMS
FOR'ARD MARCH
ORDER ARMS!
LEFT OBLIQUE MARCH!
BY THE LEFT FLANK MARCH!
COMP'NY HALT
PRESENT ARMS!

"YOU'RE IN THE ARMY NOW"

THE BITTER FATE OF HOLLAND By DEMAREE BESS

© 1941 SEPS

Preparing for War

Joining the armed forces

Although the draft was signed into law a year earlier, 1941 was a pinnacle year for the selective service program. Over 923,000 men were drafted into the military that year to meet the nation's manpower needs. The War Department's 1941 "Victory Plan" required 14 million men across all services. Originally, the act limited service to a year, but in August 1941, Congress granted the president's request to lengthen service time.

The military's ranks were not just made up of draftees. Thousands of men and women volunteered for service before the bombing of Pearl Harbor. Some were high-profile people. College football star Tom Harmon, for example, enlisted as a pilot in the Army Air Corps on Nov. 8, 1941.

Transition to military life wasn't easy. Major concerns included leaving loved ones and the rigors of training.

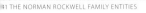

By mid-1941, the Army reached its intended strength of 1.5 million soldiers and 34 divisions.

The 1941 "Victory Plan" estimated 4 million sailors were needed to fight a two-ocean war.

Uncle Sam was a major feature in recruiting advertising in the run up to war.

Climbing an obstacle with someone draped on your back must've seemed harsh to trainees, but the lessons learned in basic training helped save lives on the battlefield.

This new crew fires 97-pound rounds from a 155-millimeter gun. Repetition and precision in training helped many soldiers to continue doing their jobs under stress.

Preparing for War

You're in the Army, now!

Whether drafted or a volunteer, Army training was the same for every man—tough. It took 13 weeks to mold a civilian into a soldier. Drill instructors would bark out orders to newbies from reveille to taps. The Army had its way of doing things, from making beds to marching in cadence. Failure to meet standards meant extra work like "KP" duty.

New soldiers were trained in firing and cleaning a rifle and how to fight as a unit. There were long marches and war games. This new life might have seemed tedious, but the routine made them soldiers. After graduation, there was a brief liberty, and then on to more advanced training such as armor, artillery or intelligence.

At San Francisco's Fort Miley, soldiers practice range finding to guide large guns located 20 miles away. Like many military jobs, this work required accuracy under pressure, as a break could turn a battle in moments.

Airborne warfare was still a relatively new concept in 1941. Despite reservations by U.S. commanders, paratroopers were vital to winning the war in Europe.

Preparing for War

Joining the Navy

In 1941, the United States Navy operated four boot camps in some beautiful locales like San Diego, but recruits weren't there to sightsee. Before being drilled and skilled, a boot would have his civilian clothes packed away, get a buzz cut, shots and Navy gear. His belongings now could be stuffed into a seabag.

For 10 weeks, recruits were put through their paces on the way to becoming sailors. They were taught seamanship, self-defense, firefighting, marksmanship, first aid, swimming and marching. The discipline was necessary. As one former sailor reported, "These things would be part of reality later on." After a graduation liberty, sailors received further training and then were deployed.

Sailors needed to get comfortable on rope ladders, as quick action might be needed to get on or off a ship.

Upon graduating from basic training, sailors were further schooled in a specific skill. These reservists are learning the ins and outs of diesel engines.

TRAIN TODAY

While you fight for tomorrow

DIESELS · SUBMARINE SERVICE

Some Navy job skills had applications beyond the military. For example, working on submarine diesels could be a plus in the job market.

Whether it was a cover illustration, a feature of a famous admiral or coverage of battles, *The Saturday Evening Post* was insightful and respectful of the Navy.

© 1941 SEPS

Squadron insignia were evocative, but there was a strict War Department protocol against maligning nations or groups.

The insignia that appeared on the cover at left represent the following squadrons:

1. Torpedo Squadron Two (VT-2) Navy
2. Scouting Squadron Forty-one (VB-41) Navy
3. Fighting Squadron Five (VF-5) Navy
4. Observation Squadron Three (VO-3) Navy
5. Torpedo Squadron Three (VT-3) Navy
6. U.S.S. Langley Navy
7. Cruiser Scouting Squadron Six (VCS-6) Navy
8. Marine Fighting Squadron Two (VMF-2) Navy
9. 99th Bombardment Squadron Army
10. U.S. Naval Air Station—Pensacola, Florida Navy
11. Cruiser Scouting Squadron Three (VCS-3) Navy
12. Scouting Squadron Seventy-one (VS-71) Navy
13. 44th Observation Squadron Army
14. Marine Scouting Squadron Two (VMS-2) Navy
15. Patrol Squadron Forty-three (VP-43) Navy
16. Scouting Squadron Six (VS-6) Navy
17. 13th Bombardment Squadron Army
18. 94th Pursuit Squadron Army
19. 90th Bombardment Squadron Army
20. 72nd Bombardment Squadron Army
21. 8th Bombardment Squadron Army
22. 26th Bombardment Squadron Army
23. 22nd Observation Squadron Army
24. Cruiser Scouting Squadron Eight (VCS-8) Navy
25. 23nd Bombardment Squadron Army
26. 11th Bombardment Squadron Army
27. Patrol Squadron 101 (VP-101) Navy
28. 55th Pursuit Squadron Army
29. 77th Pursuit Squadron Army
30. Fighting Squadron 72 (VF-72) Navy
31. 27th Pursuit Squadron Army
32. 15th Observation Squadron Army
33. 4th Reconnaissance Squadron Army
34. 95th Bombardment Squadron Army

The Metro Daily News

FINAL EDITION

NOVEMBER 26, 1941

NAGUMO'S FLEET LEAVES JAPAN FOR THE ATTACK ON PEARL HARBOR

The six-member aircraft-carrier fleet travels under strict radio silence for the surprise attack.

The Flying Line

Squadron insignia

Considering the first powered flight took place a scant 38 years earlier, warfare itself would be radically changed by aircraft on the battlefield. For instance, by the end of 1941, the newly named U.S. Army Air Forces had over 7,000 planes in operation. It would have more than 10 times the amount of planes by mid-1945. By war's end, Army, Navy and Marine aviation would grow in numbers, stature and reputation.

The era's romanticized notion of planes and pilots can be seen in the captivating nature of squadron insignia. The *Post's* cover design for Aug. 23, 1941, was a series of uniquely artistic Army and Navy squadron insignias.

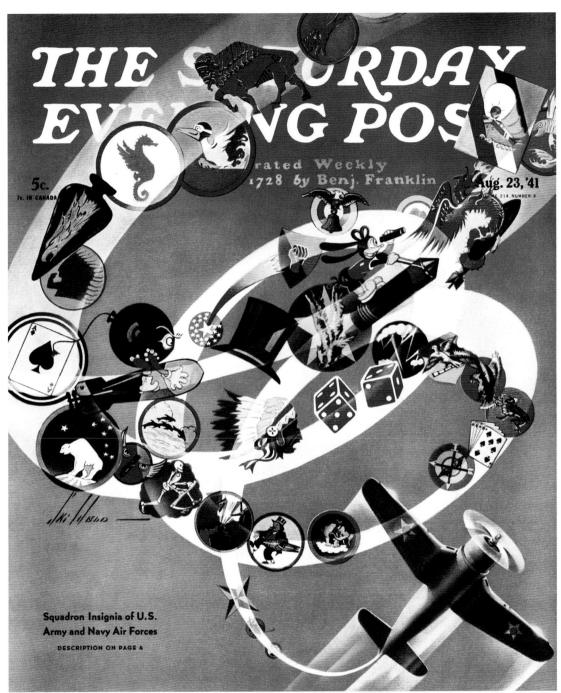

War in England

The Blitz began in the fall of 1940 as a way to soften Britain for an invasion. It continued through May 1941. London was devastated by the attacks. The nightly terror extended from as far south as Plymouth to Manchester, Liverpool and Glasgow in the north. Life was lived moment to moment. Children were evacuated whenever possible. Rationing of everything from food to clothes was the norm. A night in an air-raid shelter was a regular circumstance. Many were made homeless, children were orphaned, families killed.

Yet with typical good cheer, Britons met adversity with audacity. This island nation of 40 million unified in order to survive. Men took up arms, and women donned hard hats and marched to the factory floor. From Winston Churchill on down, the shared sacrifice assured England of its finest hour.

This 21-year old female aircraft welder was a former office worker. Hers was a typical story in 1941 England, where workplace norms and political squabbles were chucked for a single-minded unity of purpose. In a 1941 article, *Post* writer Vincent Sheehan called Britain's defense a miracle.

The Blitz officially began in the fall of 1940 and lasted until May, 1941. London took the brunt of the attacks, but other cities around the isle were attacked. Coventry, for example, was almost completely destroyed. Approximately 43,000 civilians died as a result of the bombings.

Two men sit in an air-raid shelter inside a steel mill. "But workers rarely bother to use them unless bombers are directly overhead," according to a photo caption accompanying a 1941 *Post* story entitled "They Also Fight."

The Metro Daily News

FINAL EDITION

DECEMBER 1, 1941

U.S. CIVIL AIR PATROL ESTABLISHED

Patrols set to protect nation's borders in case United States is drawn into war in Europe or the Pacific.

American aid to Britain included young men who wanted to fight against fascism. Eagle Squadrons were Royal Air Force squadrons made up of volunteers from the United States. From Feb. 5, 1941 to Sept. 29, 1942, these pilots gained experience flying against Germans before being transferred to the U.S. Army Air Forces.

Although the Lend-Lease Act was opposed by isolationists such as Charles Lindbergh, shipments of munitions and arms like these tommy guns kept Great Britain from crumbling under Axis pressure over England and in Africa.

Atlantic convoy work was a deadly, but necessary task for the United States to aid our allies. Because of the Lend-Lease policy, American destroyers and German submarines were at war months before Pearl Harbor.

War in England

We came to their aid

British forces achieved some success in 1941. The Italians were driven out of Tobruk and Libya, and the Blitz ended. The sinking of the *Bismarck* and capturing an Enigma code machine were also important.

Yet, it was the United States' Lend-Lease Act that did the most to prop up Great Britain and its allies. The act, signed in March, but with dissent from isolationists, permitted President Franklin D. Roosevelt to "sell, transfer title to, exchange, lease, lend, or otherwise dispose of, to any such government" whose defense is vital to the nation. By October, $1 billion worth of arms, munitions, ships and planes was delivered to England, which was cash-strapped and resource poor. The act was also extended to aid Russia, France, China and other allies.

In July, Roosevelt and Prime Minister Winston Churchill met for the first time and agreed to a joint declaration against fascism. The Atlantic Charter outlined a democratic world.

Fitters are at work assembling an American light tank which arrived at an English ordnance depot from the United States as part of a Lend-Lease shipment in 1941.

FAMOUS BIRTHDAYS
Beau Bridges, December 9 actor
John Davidson, December 13
singer and actor

Japanese ambassador Kichisaburo Nomura (left), U.S. Secretary of State Cordell Hull and Japanese envoy Dr. Saburo Kurusu soberly stroll on White House grounds during negotiations in November 1941.

Pearl Harbor

December 7, 1941

By November 1941, diplomatic activity between the two nations had all but ended. Japanese expansion had consumed large sections of Asia, cutting off vital resources to the West.

Months prior to the diplomatic impasse, Japanese Adm. Isoroku Yamamoto, commander of the Japanese fleet, had begun training pilots for the attack on Pearl Harbor. By Oct. 1, 1941 the Japanese high command gave its approval of the attack. On Nov. 26, Adm. Chuichi Nagumo's task force of six carriers and numerous support ships left Japan.

At 6 a.m., Dec. 7, Nagumo launched 181 planes from his six carriers. Two hours later, the Japanese strike force reigned down bombs on the U.S. fleet at Pearl Harbor as well as military airfields across the islands. Where moments earlier sailors were observing a Sunday morning in paradise, "Battleship Row" was now an inferno with the fleet's dreadnaughts burning and sinking. America was at war.

A Japanese Navy Type 97 attack plane, known as a "Kate," takes off from a carrier as one of 170 fighters and bombers that made up the second wave of attack on the U.S. Pacific Fleet at Pearl Harbor.

A picture from a Japanese pilot: a view of "Battleship Row" at about 8:00 a.m. on Dec. 7, 1941. USS ships are, from lower left to right: Nevada; Arizona; Tennessee with West Virginia outboard; Maryland with Oklahoma outboard; and California. West Virginia, Oklahoma and California have been torpedoed. Hickam Field is ablaze in the background.

Part of the Japanese strategy was to suppress any attempts by the U.S. military to launch a counter-attack against the swarms of fighters and bombers. In the first wave of the assault, the Japanese attacked the airfields at Hickman, Wheeler, Ford Island, Ewa and Kaneohe. Ironically, minutes before the attack, a newly installed radar station mistook the Japanese aircraft as a group of B-17s flying in from the mainland, so fighters weren't scrambled.

At 8 a.m., Dec. 7, the USS *West Virginia* was moored on the outside of the USS *Tennessee*. The Japanese struck the USS *West Virginia* with several aerial bombs and torpedoes before the battleship settled to the harbor bottom. There is some evidence from the U.S. Naval Institute that she may have also been struck by a torpedo launched from a midget submarine. The USS *West Virginia* was refloated in May 1942. After extensive modernization, she rejoined the fleet in 1944.

Thick smoke from the destroyer USS *Shaw* silhouettes a smoldering USS *Nevada*, which was one of the battleships prized by the Japanese aircrews. The USS *Nevada* was the only battlewagon able to get underway during the attack, but she had to be beached after taking hits from bombs and a torpedo. The USS *Nevada* returned to combat in May 1943. The battleship was redeployed to the Atlantic, where it took part in the Normandy invasion, before returning to action in the Pacific.

Despite damage, the USS *California* nearly got underway before she was blocked by a mass of burning oil. She eventually sank to the harbor bottom.

Pearl Harbor

A day which will live in infamy

The USS *West Virginia* was the first to go. The USS *Oklahoma* rolled over and sank soon after. At 8:10, the USS *Arizona* exploded and sank, killing 1,177 sailors—nearly half of all American's killed in the attack. Within the first half hour of the assault, the USS battleships *California*, *Maryland*, *Tennessee* and *Nevada* were badly damaged.

Waves of Japanese planes went after U.S. airfields. Bombers cratered runways and destroyed planes on the ground. Fighters strafed soldiers.

The attack ended at 10 a.m. American losses were staggering. Twenty-one ships were either sunk or damaged. Over 300 airplanes were either destroyed or put out of action. There were 2,403 dead and 1,178 wounded. Cold comfort could be taken from the fact the U.S. carriers were already out to sea.

Black smoke from the USS *California* conceals the capsized USS *Oklahoma*. The USS *California* was raised from the harbor bottom, repaired and redeployed to the Pacific Fleet in 1944. The USS *Oklahoma* was raised, but wasn't salvaged. The USS *Arizona* remains as a memorial in Pearl Harbor.

When the Japanese struck Pearl Harbor, the USS *Arizona* was moored next to her repair ship. Several direct hits by bombs ravaged the ship. Explosions and fires blew out her sides. Her turrets, conning tower and much of her superstructure fell into the hull. She sank, killing 1,177 sailors. This ship was a symbol of the day's savagery and heroism under fire.

United States Enters the War

"Delay invites danger," is what Roosevelt told Congress when he asked for and received a declaration of war against Germany on Dec. 11.

"Yesterday, Dec. 7, 1941—a date which will live in infamy—the United States of America was suddenly and deliberately attacked by naval and air forces of the Empire of Japan." Thus began one of the seminal speeches in American history, as President Franklin D. Roosevelt asked a joint session of Congress to declare war against Japan. In his short address, Roosevelt galvanized a shocked nation when he affirmed: "With confidence in our armed forces—with the unbounded determination of our people—we will gain the inevitable triumph—so help us God." Roosevelt signed the war declaration just hours after the speech.

On Dec. 11, Roosevelt signed a war declaration against Germany. Roosevelt's oratory and leadership was met with great support. Men flooded military recruitment offices. Civilians manned barricades. Bonds were bought. People sacrificed to save the nation.

War bonds could be purchased outright or through payroll deduction. By the time sales ended, more than $185 billion worth of bonds was sold.

© BETTMANN/CORBIS.

With Vice President Henry A. Wallace (left, behind podium) and Speaker of the House Sam Rayburn looking on, Roosevelt asked for swift Congressional action in declaring war on Japan. The president signed the declaration at 4 p.m. on Dec. 8.

SAN FRANCISCO HISTORY CENTER, SAN FRANCISCO PUBLIC LIBRARY

Fairmont Hotel manager Bernard Leonard and Barbara Bliss of the San Francisco aircraft warning service work with two soldiers on sealing large windows to keep out shattered glass and bomb fragments. Tension was high weeks after Pearl Harbor, as Americans expected a surprise attack on West Coast cities like San Francisco.

SAN FRANCISCO HISTORY CENTER, SAN FRANCISCO PUBLIC LIBRARY

These young men give "thumbs up" salute at a recruitment station set up at San Francisco's Palace Hotel. Military enlistment soared in the days and weeks after Pearl Harbor.

Defending Our Freedom

In 1941, as war appeared inevitable, Americans embraced the principals inscribed in the country's founding documents. In this Nov. 15, 1941 ad in the *Post*, Goodyear placed itself as both a believer in the American ideals of liberty and justice, and a willing partner in protecting those freedoms. The ad reads as follows:

There is the right of a man to stand on his own two feet, and with his own hands and talents carve out a place for himself and his family.

There is the right of a woman to look hopefully ahead, to raise up her brood in dignity and self-respect, undictated to, save by her own mother-wisdom and conscience.

There is the right of a boy to lead the hale, free life of boys, flying kites when the wind blows, playing cops and robbers when he wants, going to school when he must—and out of it all, somehow shaping future to a good pattern.

There is the right of a small child to its chance for health and love and laughter, to a good start toward who-knows-what fine and useful life in years to come.

Simple things, aren't they, these things that spell America and add up to freedom! So simple, so wholesome, it seems daft that somewhere bombs scream down to blast them, tanks lunge to crush them, bullets fly to drive from the minds of men the idea that these are their rights, inalienable. But the bombs do fall, the tanks do roll, the bullets do fly—and in such a world, our only shield seems to be more bombs of our own with bombers to carry them, more tanks and the cannon to arm them, more bullets and faster guns to fire them.

So it is that from Goodyear factories meant for building things to enlarge life and make it better, now must flow in a swelling tide the things our country needs if we are to hold what we have. Skills and facilities developed that a peaceful world might have better tires, floor coverings, soles and heels, transmission belts and a thousand like useful things, now focus on the making of barrage balloons, bomber wings and tails, bullet-puncture-sealing inner tubes and fuel tanks, gas masks, rubber tank track treads and a host of other Goodyear-made defense products.

This is no choice of ours—like yourself, we would far rather spend our days making this a land where life can be richer, liberty enjoyed, where the pursuit of happiness can go steadily on. But when the decision lies between helping our government prepare for impregnable defense of such things, or running the risk of having them swept away, there is no option, and we feel as we know you do. That is why, for the time being, some Goodyear dealers may not have in stock the particular size and kind of Goodyear tire you want—simply because, that which we in America have, we intend to do our part to hold. Compared with holding it, what else matters?

More *The Saturday Evening Post Covers*

The Saturday Evening Post covers were works of art, many illustrated by famous artists of the time, including Norman Rockwell. Most of the 1941 covers have been incorporated within the previous pages of this book; the few that were not are presented on the following pages for your enjoyment.

POLAND IN CHAINS By DEMAREE BESS

MORE FAMOUS BIRTHDAYS

January 4
John Bennett Perry, actor

January 7
John E. Walker, English chemist, Nobel Prize laureate

January 9
Joan Baez, singer and activitist

January 11
Jimmy Velvit, rock 'n' roll singer/songwriter

January 15
Captain Beefheart, singer/songwriter

January 21
Richie Havens, musician

January 24
Aaron Neville, singer

January 26
Scott Glenn, actor

January 30
Dick Cheney, former vice president of the United States

January 31
Dick Gephardt, politician

February 1
Jerry Spinelli, children's author

February 3
Dory Funk Jr., professional wrestler

February 4
John Steel, drummer (The Animals)

February 5
David Selby, actor
Barrett Strong, singer and songwriter

February 6
Howard Phillips, politician
Dave Berry, British pop singer

February 8
Tom Rush, folk and blues singer

February 11
Sérgio Mendes, Latin American musician

February 15
Brian Holland, songwriter/producer

February 18
Irma Thomas, soul singer

February 19
David Gross, physicist, Nobel Prize laureate

February 24
Joanie Sommers, singer and actress

March 6
Palle Mikkelborg, jazz trumpeter and composer

March 8
Ivana Loudová, composer

March 15
Mike Love, singer/songwriter (The Beach Boys)

March 16
Chuck Woolery, game show host

March 17
Paul Kantner, rock guitarist

March 23
Jim Trelease, educator and author

March 28
Jim Turner, football placekicker

March 29
Joseph Hooton Taylor Jr., astrophysicist, Nobel Prize laureate

April 3
Jan Berry, of surf-music duo Jan & Dean

April 9
Kaye Adams, country singer
Jerome M. Antil, author

April 13
Michael Stuart Brown, geneticist, recipient of the Nobel Prize in Physiology or Medicine

April 14
Julie Christie, British actress
Pete Rose, baseball player

April 19
Roberto Carlos, singer/composer

April 27
Lee Roy Jordan, football player

April 28
K. Barry Sharpless, chemist, Nobel Prize laureate

May 11
Eric Burdon, vocalist (The Animals)

May 13
Senta Berger, Austrian actress
Ritchie Valens, singer
Joe Brown, singer and guitarist

May 15
K.T. Oslin, musician

May 19
Bobby Burgess, dancer and singer
Nora Ephron, film producer, director and screenwriter

May 31
Louis J. Ignarro, pharmacologist, recipient of the Nobel Prize in Physiology or Medicine

June 1
Edo de Waart, conductor

June 2
William Guest, singer (Gladys Knight & the Pips)
Charlie Watts, drummer (The Rolling Stones)

June 5
Spalding Gray, actor and screenwriter
Martha Argerich, pianist

June 8
Fuzzy Haskins, musician

June 9
Jon Lord, organist of Deep Purple

June 10
James A. Paul, writer and nonprofit executive
Shirley Owens, singer (The Shirelles)

June 12
Marv Albert, sports announcer

June 21
Joe Flaherty, American-Canadian actor

June 22
Michael Lerner, actor

June 24
Bill Reardon, politician and educator

July 5
Terry Cashman, record producer and singer-songwriter

July 14
Maulana Karenga, author and activist

July 18
Martha Reeves, vocalist
Lonnie Mack, rock and blues guitarist

July 19
Vikki Carr, singer

July 28
Riccardo Muti, conductor

August 2
Doris Coley, singer (The Shirelles)

August 3
Beverly Lee, singer (The Shirelles)

August 6
Lyle Berman, professional poker player

August 14
Connie Smith, country singer
David Crosby, singer/songwriter

September 10
Christopher Hogwood, conductor and harpsichordist

September 13
David Clayton-Thomas, vocalist

September 14
Alberto Naranjo, arranger and composer

September 15
George Saimes, football player

September 20
Dale Chihuly, glass sculptor

September 24
Guy Hovis, singer

October 3
Chubby Checker, singer

October 4
Elizabeth Eckford, activist
Anne Rice, writer
Roy Blount Jr., writer and comedian

October 10
Peter Coyote, actor

October 16
Tim McCarver, baseball commentator

October 17
James Seals, musician, singer/songwriter (Seals and Crofts)
Alan Howard, bassist (The Tremeloes)

October 23
Mel Winkler, actor

October 25
Helen Reddy, Australian singer and actress
Anne Tyler, novelist

October 30
Otis Williams, vocalist

November 1
Robert Foxworth, actor

November 2
Brian Poole, singer (The Tremeloes)
Bruce Welch, guitarist and singer

November 8
Simon Standage, baroque violinist

November 9
Tom Fogerty, guitarist (Creedence Clearwater Revival)

November 21
David Porter, soul musician

December 2
Tom McGuinness, guitarist (Manfred Mann)

December 18
Prince William of Gloucester, grandson of George V

December 19
Maurice White, singer/songwriter, musician & record producer (Earth, Wind & Fire)

December 27
Les Maguire, pianist (Gerry & the Pacemakers)
Mike Pinder, English rock musician (The Moody Blues)

December 29
Ray Thomas, English musician, singer and composer (The Moody Blues)

December 30
Mel Renfro, football player

Facts and Figures of 1941

President of the U.S.
Franklin D. Roosevelt
Vice President of the U.S.
Henry A. Wallace

Population of the U.S.
133,407,000

Births
2,703,000

College Graduates
Males: 103,889
Females: 81,457

Average Salary for full-time employee: $1,462.00
Minimum Wage (per hour): $0.30

© BETTMANN/CORBIS

Average cost for:

Bread (lb.) $0.08

Bacon (lb.) $0.34

Butter (lb.) $0.41

Eggs (doz.) $0.40

Milk (gal.)..............................$0.54

Potatoes (10 lbs.)..................$0.24

Coffee (lb.) $0.24

Sugar (5 lb.) $0.29

Gasoline (gal.)......................$0.12

Movie Ticket.......................$0.25

Postage Stamp.....................$0.03

Car..$850.00

Single-Family Home .. $4,075.00

1941
AMERICAN
AIRLINES

Notable Inventions and Firsts

January 22: Grand Coulee Dam in Washington state goes into operation.

February 7: Frank Sinatra and Tommy Dorsey Orchestra record "Everything Happens to Me."

March 1: The first U.S. commercial FM radio station goes on the air in Nashville, Tenn.

March 3: Forest Mars patents a process to create hard-shelled chocolate candies, calling them M&Ms. Their hard shells enable the candies to withstand heat, a feature that wins them popularity among U.S. servicemen and leads to the slogan, "The milk chocolate that melts in your mouth—not in your hands."

April 26: A tradition begins at Wrigley Field in Chicago: For the first time, an organ is played at a baseball game.

May 1: General Mills introduces Cheerios.

June: The U.S. Navy needed an all-purpose, lightweight building that could be shipped anywhere and assembled without skilled labor. The George A. Fuller construction company was selected to manufacture what became the Quonset hut. The first was produced within 60 days of contract award. The first shipment was transported by the Navy in June.

Sports Winners

NCAA Basketball Championship: Wisconsin defeats Washington State
NFL: Chicago Bears defeat New York Giants
World Series: New York Yankees defeat Brooklyn Dodgers
Stanley Cup: Boston Bruins defeat Detroit Red Wings
The Masters: Craig Wood wins
PGA Championship: Victor J. Ghezzi wins
Kentucky Derby Champion: Whirlaway

September 2: The Academy of Motion Pictures Arts and Sciences copyrights Oscar statuette.

September 27: The first Liberty ship, the SS *Patrick Henry*, is launched at Baltimore, Md.

October 30: Franklin Delano Roosevelt approves $1 billion in Lend-Lease aid to the Soviet Union.

November 10: In a speech at the Mansion House in London, Winston Churchill promises, "should the United States become involved in war with Japan, the British declaration will follow within the hour."

November 21: The radio program *King Biscuit Time* is broadcast for the first time (it later becomes the longest running daily radio broadcast in history and the most famous live blues radio program).

December 5: Sister Elizabeth Kenny's new treatment for infantile paralysis, polio, approved by U.S. medicine.

December 22: The comic strip *Archie* first appears, created by New York writer and pulp magazine publisher John L. Goldwater, 25, with help from teenaged artist Bob Montana. Archie, Jughead, Reggie, Betty, Veronica and their teenaged friends live in suburban Riverdale, U.S.A.

1941 ETHYL CORPORATION/NEW MARKET CORP.

Live It Again 1941

PROJECT EDITOR	Barb Sprunger
ART DIRECTOR	Brad Snow
COPYWRITERS	Jill Case, Jim Langham
COPY SUPERVISOR	Deborah Morgan
PRODUCTION ARTIST SUPERVISOR	Erin Augsburger
PRODUCTION ARTIST	Erin Augsburger
COPY EDITOR	Mary O'Donnell
PHOTOGRAPHY SUPERVISOR	Tammy Christian
NOSTALGIA EDITOR	Ken Tate
EDITORIAL DIRECTOR	Jeanne Stauffer
PUBLISHING SERVICES DIRECTOR	Brenda Gallmeyer

Printed in China
First Printing: 2011
Library of Congress Number: 2010904350
ISBN: 978-1-59217-307-5

Customer Service
LiveItAgain.com
(800) 829-5865

1 2 3 4 5 6 7 8 9